Wild About Brass

Inspiring, effective teaching resources

Ruth Wild

For backing tracks visit:

www.musicwild.co.uk and go to the 'Wild About Brass' tab

Acknowledgement from the author
I would like to thank my husband, Stephen Wild, without whose expertise, time, energy and support, this book would not exist.

ISBN: 979-8-7722-6590-1

Design: riverdesignbooks.com

Contents

Introduction:
The Thinking Behind *Wild About Brass*

Independent Learning

One of our most important objectives as teachers is to enable our pupils to develop independence. What does that mean exactly for instrumental music teachers, and how will this book help?

The list below shows the characteristics of independent learners in the context of instrumental music.

Independent instrumental music learners:

- can listen for themselves, think for themselves, make musical decisions (create), so that:
  - they have a clear idea of an intended sound, recognise if they have played a sound other than that which is intended, and understand how to adjust it accordingly
  - they consider the effects of playing something in different ways, and form opinions about what sounds better
  - they can make up their own musical material using the notes they know how to play
  - they are able to learn music in different ways, including with and without notation

- can adapt to:
  - playing in different situations (such as a new ensemble)
  - playing in different sound worlds, such as music from different periods or genres

- are motivated to:
  - attend the next lesson
  - improve
  - practise between lessons
  - attend an ensemble
  - carry on playing when they leave school

I am sure that we can all recognise these attributes as beneficial for our pupils. Our role as teachers is vital in helping pupils achieve them.

We need to:

- enable pupils to listen and think for themselves, and to make musical decisions
- nurture pupils' curiosity for different sound worlds and equip them with the necessary musical tools
- ensure pupils are motivated, understanding and addressing any social and psychological issues that may affect their willingness to try something and to pursue it.

Wild About Brass contains activities that encourage learners to listen and think for themselves. Aural activities are largely played on the instrument, and wherever possible use real music – pieces rather than exercises. As most activities are played on the instrument, they are particularly effective in encouraging pupils to listen and evaluate their own playing (including, for instance, spotting when they have played an incorrect pitch, and self-correcting). I have included non-notated activities, which provide opportunities for pupils to focus more on listening and less on looking. This means that their attention will be more easily directed towards the evaluation of their own playing. Activities also help learners to make musical decisions – these come in the form of improvising, interpreting and arranging.

Wild About Brass will help you provide pupils with a good foundation in a comprehensive range of skills, including aural, creative, and notation. Pupils will develop their ability to learn music in different ways, be it from notation or without. This will enable them to participate in a diverse range of ensembles.

Wild About Brass will equip you to teach pupils an ensemble piece without notation. This will allow them to be more receptive to their fellow musicians. By regularly playing without notation, pupils will increase their aural awareness, developing their capacity to absorb stylistic differences between music of different periods, places and genres. This book will ensure that your pupils have the necessary musical tools to explore and enjoy a range of sound worlds.

Wild About Brass will help pupils realise that they are making progress. Experience has shown me that all pupils have the potential to enjoy learning and performing music in different ways. It is true that pupils sometimes appear in the first instance to have less aptitude or motivation in a particular area. However, this is often due to a lack of self-belief; they attribute a perceived lack of success to something about themselves that they can't change. Activities from this book will gently guide them through the different ways of playing music in easy step-by-step stages.

Wild About Brass has detailed explanations of how to teach the activities. We as teachers may feel under-confident in a particular area of making music – be it playing *with* notation, *without* notation, or improvising. With this in mind I have described the activities clearly and simply, with many 'Points to Note' and 'Top Tips.'

Learning Through Playing

The activities in **Wild About Brass** are mostly played on pupils' instruments. Using the voice and body percussion can be very helpful, and some activities include these strategies. But in weekly instrumental lessons, often the best way to develop generic musical skills – general musicianship - is through playing. The reasons for this are practical, musical and educational, as shown below:

- Holistic learning. Musicians need to listen and create *whilst* playing. The activities we use with pupils need to reflect this. It is useful to remember too, that technical skills may be developed and consolidated by carrying out well-chosen aural and creative activities on the instrument.

- The suitability of the music. Specific characteristics of a piece of music may lend themselves more readily to playing than singing.

- Psychological or physiological problems pupils have in relation to singing. Some pupils may find it more comfortable to play.

- Pupils want to play. In the context of instrumental lessons and ensemble rehearsals pupils' primary motivation is playing their instrument.

- Practicalities. Instrumental lessons are often short. Learning aural and creative skills through playing is normally a better use of time.

Real Music Making

One of the best things we can do to motivate learners is to ensure that there is real music making in every lesson. Pupils love to feel that they are participating in music making where the primary purpose is to express and evoke emotion. Even at an early stage, learners are aware that a piece can be musically satisfying. Therefore, activities in the book are as far as possible pieces of music rather than exercises, games or warm-ups - including those concerned with general musicianship, for example, aural and creative activities. Aural skills are developed by working out pieces by ear, or learning pieces by rote. Creative skills are developed by interpreting and arranging pieces, and by creating melodies. Improvising is made to feel like proper music making even with beginners, by the use of attractive backing tracks.

How to integrate the activities with pupils' other learning

Pupils need to learn and develop a broad range of skills. The best way to do this is simultaneously, with no skill left behind. In WCET[1] and ensembles, where sessions normally last a reasonably long time this is relatively straightforward. However, in individual and small group lessons this can be daunting. Given that lessons are short – often no more than twenty minutes - you may worry about how to include aural and creative activities. Will technique be neglected? How will activities fit with a pupil's tutor book?

In **Wild About Brass** I give advice about how to use the activities in lessons, bearing in mind time constraints, and that the natural flow of the lesson still needs to happen: hearing what has been practised; helping the pupil to develop and consolidate skills; preparing the pupil for subsequent practice. I indicate where activities are better used as parts of lessons – in which case I recommend how to divide up the learning – and where they may be used to cover an entire lesson.

Activities are centred around key stages of learning: when the first two notes are learnt; when the first five notes of a major scale can be played; when the whole of a major scale can be played. This means that the technical matters associated with these stages can be developed and consolidated - for example, moving between one note and its neighbour can be practised, not only by a piece from a tutor book, but by using the activities from the first section of **Wild About Brass**. As activities are largely played on the instrument, this increases the opportunities to hone technical points.

It is clear which notes are used in the activities. This ensures that it is easy to determine which stage of a tutor book they correspond to.

Notation activities will improve pupils' ability to read pieces from their tutor books.

At each stage of **Wild About Brass** pupils learn an ensemble part for the tune 'La Bourrée Occitane.' These can be put together for performance using single instruments (for example trumpets), or mixed brass.

---

[1] Whole Class Ensemble Teaching – or 'Wider Opportunities'

What Can We Do with Two Notes?

Activities use **C** and **D** for all brass instruments. You might want to use **F** and **G** if your beginner players find that the higher notes are easier to produce. Other notes are fine to use, too – whichever suit you and your learners. If your learners are naming the notes as if in the bass clef (for trombone and tuba), then this is an easy matter to accommodate. This book will assume that **C** and **D** are two notes which are playable.

For backing tracks visit:
www.musicwild.co.uk and
go to the
'Wild About Brass' tab

N.B. If you have a mixed group of brass, E flat instruments will play the same sounding pitches as B flat instruments if the E flat players use C and D, and the B flat players use F and G. Similarly, B flat players and F players can combine if the F horn players use F and G, and the B flat players use C and D. Other combinations can be catered for if different starting notes are chosen, and all the examples can be transposed as needed to facilitate this.

Activity 1: Echo Playing

*see audio links nos. 1a)i) & 1a)ii) - in Bb, 1b)i) & 1b)ii) - in Eb, and 1c)i) & 1c)ii) - in F. *

Play phrases of 2 bars in 4/4 using C and D (or whichever pitches you have chosen), for pupils to copy back.

Top tips:

- Tell pupils which note your first phrase will start on. You may wish to use just one note for your first phrase.

- Be prepared to repeat a phrase if a pupil isn't successful first time.

- Ensure pupils work out the notes with aural clues - not visual clues from your instrument, such as valves used or slide position. This can be achieved by standing behind pupils, or by asking them to face different parts of the room. If space doesn't allow for this (e.g. in the case of large groups), you can sing the phrases to be copied. If you do this, bear in mind that pupils *may* be slightly confused by the fact that your voice has a different timbre to their instrument. (Singing at a different octave to the instrument doesn't normally cause any additional problems for your pupils.)

* tracks labelled i) include phrases for pupils to copy back, so facilitate home practice;
  tracks labelled ii) contain just the backing, giving the teacher more flexibility in lessons.

Supplementary exercise for differentiating pitch.

Some of your pupils may not yet believe they can differentiate between pitches: the idea is too abstract for them – they haven't yet learnt that their ears can give them the relevant information. If this is the case, follow the steps below:

- Demonstrate what we mean by high and low in music by showing some extreme examples – a very high note, and a very low note.

- Play one note repeatedly then change to an adjacent one (e.g. C to D). Ask pupils to show that they have spotted the change in pitch with a hand gesture – simply low hand for low pitch, high hand for high pitch. Repeat, ensuring that pupils are using their ears, and not following any visual clues, such as from your instrument, or from another pupil. You can do this by, for instance, standing behind them or asking them to face different parts of the room.

- Pupils will easily recognise the change in sound, and this will help them realise that they can recognise changes in pitch.

- As pupils improve at this, oscillate between the two pitches, becoming more rapid for greater challenge, and to add fun, though never exceeding pupils' ability to accomplish the task.

Activity 2: Improvising - Riff and Rest, Riff and Play

see audio links nos. 2a) – in B flat, 2b) – in E flat, and 2c) – in F. A 'tutti' phrase is included.

- Decide on a 2 bar phrase in 4/4 using C and D. Teach it to your pupils aurally. (See example on p.12.)

- Ask pupils to play the phrase, then leave a gap of the same length, then play the same phrase again, in other words: 2 bar phrase, 2 bars rest, 2 bar phrase. Do this on a loop. Pupils can count 1 2 3 4|1 2 3 4 for the bars' rest, or use fun words such as hot po-ta-to, hot po-ta-to. Pupils' own names, food or animals might be sources for the words.

- Importantly, learners now need to internalise that phrase length. Ask them to repeat the actions in the last bullet point, but now counting in their heads, not out loud. Then ask them to repeat with no visual clues from you or their fellow learners. They might, for instance, turn to face away from each other.

- Next fill the gap with your own improvisations, choosing from the same notes, and demonstrating at least some improvisations that are very simple – perhaps just a rhythm on one of the notes and some rests. Learners are now playing the phrase all together, listening to your improvisation, playing the phrase all together, and so on.

- Ask learners to fill in the gaps with their own improvisations. They will now be playing the same phrase all together, followed by their own improvisations, followed by the same phrase all together. Continue to do this on a loop. It is good that they get more than one chance at improvising.

Top tips:

- The process can be broken into small chunks – perhaps a bullet point or two at a time - then returned to the following lesson.

- You don't need to use the term improvisation specifically. 'Make up your own tune' or 'pattern' will suffice with less experienced pupils.

- Remind learners that simple improvisations are often the best, and that they only need to use the two notes (C and D). Choosing just one note at this stage is fine if that's what they want.

- You should always join in with the 'tutti' phrase (the one they all play) at the right time – exactly after two bars has elapsed, even if some pupils seem to be over- or under-running with their improvisations. It is vital that the sense of pulse is maintained and that learners continue to internalise the correct phrase length.

- If you have a group, start to ask smaller numbers of learners at a time to improvise. In a class or ensemble situation you can split into small groups by, for instance, asking what they had for lunch. Those who had sandwiches can do the first improvisation, those who had chips can do the second improvisation and so on. Next ask if any pairs of pupils would like to improvise together, and finally ask for solos. Avoid going down a line asking for solo improvisations in a large group – it can be quite stressful waiting for your turn!

Example:

Hot   po - ta - to   Hot   po - ta - to

Count out loud then....
Count in heads then.....
Count in heads no visual clues

Next...........................

Teacher improvises...............

Hot   po - ta - to   Hot   po - ta - to

Then..............................

Pupils improvise.....................

Supplementary aural/rhythm activity for differentiating crotchets and minims:

- Choose some words for: 4 crotchets; 2 minims; a minim and 2 crotchets; 2 crotchets and a minim. Food and pets are popular themes. You might have chick-en tikk-a (4 crotchets), baked beans (2 minims), cheese sand-wich (minim + 2 crotchets) and fish and chips (2 crotchets + minim). Ensure the words will produce the desired rhythms when chanted, so for instance 'choc'late cake' only works for 2 crotchets then a minim, not a minim then 2 crotchets.

- Show pupils how to play the rhythms with the words. Stick to one pitch. Use one of the notes from the previous activity.

- Choose one of the rhythms, for example, cheese sand-wich, and play it without telling pupils which one you have chosen, i.e. they hear the notes but don't know which words they represent – they have to work it out. If a pupil answers correctly, they have a chance to choose one of the rhythms to play for the other pupils to work out. (In individual lessons they can play to you.) In small groups you can ensure that all pupils have a go eventually.

- To make the activity harder, play two rhythms consecutively, for example, cheese sand-wich + chick-en tikk-a, or fish and chips + fish and chips.

Activity 3: Working Out By Ear

- Sing the first phrase of Happy Birthday to You starting on C.

- Sing just the first two notes, and ask pupils if they are the same or different. Sometimes pupils are confused because the syllables are different, so feel that there has been a change of pitch too. If that is the case try playing the first two notes standing behind them, so that they can't see you or your instrument (pupils need to work this out aurally, not visually). They will normally then realise that the two notes are the same.

- Say that the first note is a C, and establish that therefore both notes are C.

- Now sing or play the first three notes. Ask if the third note is the same as the first two or different. When pupils have established that it is different, ask if it is higher or lower than the first two notes.

- When pupils have established that the next note is higher, ask them what it could be. Ask pupils to try out their suggestions so that they can confirm whether or not their answer is correct.

- Once it is established that the next note is D, sing or play the first *four* notes and ask pupils to work out if the last two notes are the same or different, lower or higher. Again, invite them to try out their ideas to confirm whether their answer is correct.

Top tips:

- If pupils are finding it difficult to differentiate pitch, use the supplementary exercise under Activity 1: Echo Playing.

- Always ensure pupils are working out the notes aurally, i.e. without visual clues.

Activity 4: Learning a Tune Without notation – La Bourrée Occitane

see audio link nos. 3 score, 3i) part 1, 3ii) part 2, 3iii) part 3, and 3iv) part 4.

See score for La Bourrée on p.16. For pupils playing two notes refer to the fourth line of the stave.

Explain to pupils that for this piece, their tummies will be the note C and their shoulders will be D

Help pupils to remember the rhythm of the tune by using some fun words. See below:

Tummies..Shoulders.................................etc.

I've had some toast   with jam and butt - er   spread all   ov - er.

A small section at a time, ask learners to:

- Tap the relevant body part – tummy for C, shoulders for D - in the rhythm of the tune, whilst saying the fun words (demonstrate first)
- Tap relevant body parts whilst *saying* the *note names*
- Tap relevant body parts whilst *singing* the *note names*
- Tap relevant body parts whilst *thinking* the *note names*
- Play that section

Try small sections at a time like this, then gradually join sections together until all the piece can be performed.

Play Part 1 whilst they play Part 4. If they find this difficult you can go back to small sections at a time and/or ask them to tap their part temporarily before going back to playing.

Top tips:

- A stamp can be included at the beginning of bar 5, and a shouted 'hoi' on the second beat of bar 12. These will help maintain a good pulse. They can be retained for performance or transferred to 'thinking voice.'

- You can also ask pupils to think of their own words. Ask them to choose a theme, such as food, pets, football teams and film characters. Tap the rhythm of sections of the tune and see if they can think of some words to fit.

- Unless pupils have access to a recording of the music it will be difficult for them to practise the material at home. If that is the case devote a comparatively small proportion of the lesson to learning the piece and return to it the following week. This will ensure you have enough time to spend on what *will* be practised for the following lesson.

- Using the same principles, arrange your own pieces to suit your pupils.

Activity 5: Arranging and Interpreting – La Bourrée Occitane

- Once your pupils can play their part in La Bourrée Occitane along with the melody, ask them to try it with different articulations and dynamics (within the limits of their technical capability). Invite them to make a judgement on which sounds best.

- If playing the piece as an ensemble with all parts invite pupils to think of an introduction. For example, any of the parts could play the 'A' part (bars 1 to 8) three times, with other parts joining in after the first time around.

Activity 6: Notation and Aural

Please see the pitch cards provided on pages 20 to 27. There are four for the notes C and D, and four for F and G.

- Play card no. 2. Then look at card no. 1. Discuss how the last two notes of card no. 1 look different – that they are higher up the stave than the first two notes. Explain that if a note looks higher, it will sound higher (see Top tips*). Given that the first two notes are both C (or F), ask pupils what the last two notes might be. Having established that they are D (or G), play the card. Ensure pupils have noted where the 'blob' on the note D (or G) is. In other words, for D it is just underneath the bottom line. (In the case of G the second line up goes through the blob.) Work out and play the other cards.

- Play all four cards in a row. Shuffle them and play in a different order.

- Play a card and ask pupils to work out which one you played. Ensure pupils are using aural clues, not visual, so stand behind them, or sing the card. The individual who identifies the correct card first gets the chance to play a card for the rest of the group to identify. Ensure all have a go at this, so you can use the rule that if a pupil has already answered one, got it right and played, they should miss the next turn(s). This shouldn't take long with a small group, so no pupil should be waiting long. Again, ensure that pupils are working out the notes their friends are playing by aural rather than visual means. This works well for individual pupils too – just alternate who is playing and who is working out the answer.

Top tips:

- For best results photocopy the notes onto card and laminate. For PDF versions of the pitch cards visit www.musicwild.co.uk and go to the 'Wild About Brass' tab: 'Pitch cards.'

- *Pupils should by now understand how the words 'higher' and 'lower' are used in music with regard to pitch. If not, return to the supplementary exercise after Activity 1: Echo Playing.

Practical considerations for WCET:

- You may want to photocopy the notes onto different coloured card – a different colour for each card. This ensures pupils can refer easily to a particular card, for instance, 'the yellow one' rather than 'the third one from the left' etc.

- Ask for volunteers to hold up the cards in a row. Choose pupils who you noticed have grasped the point well so that you can concentrate on checking learners who didn't initially understand.

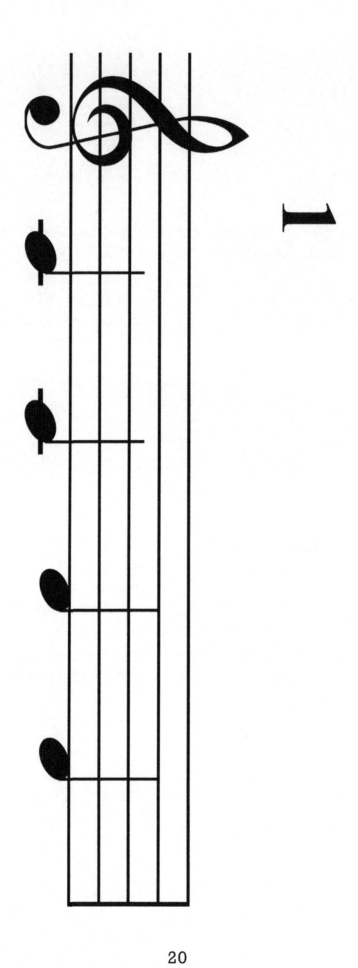

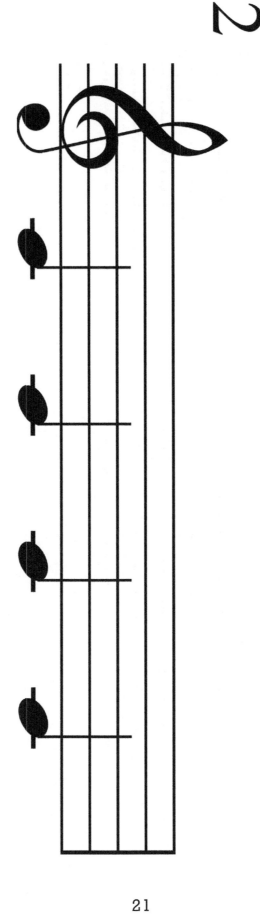

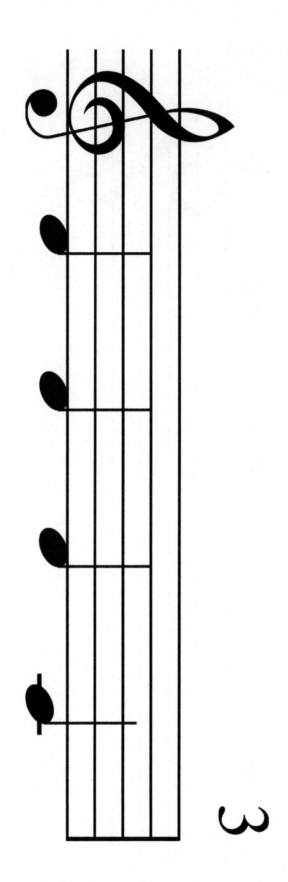

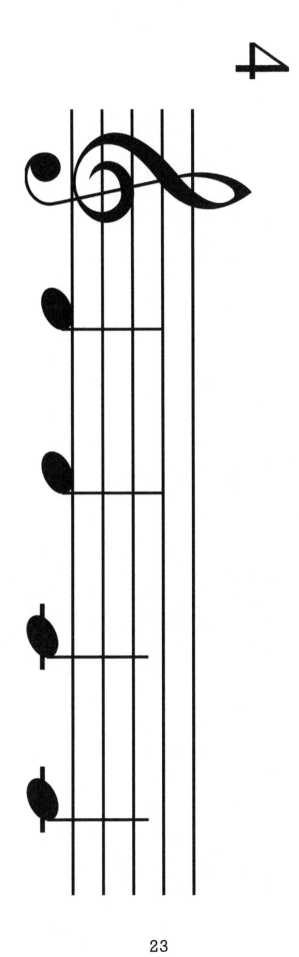

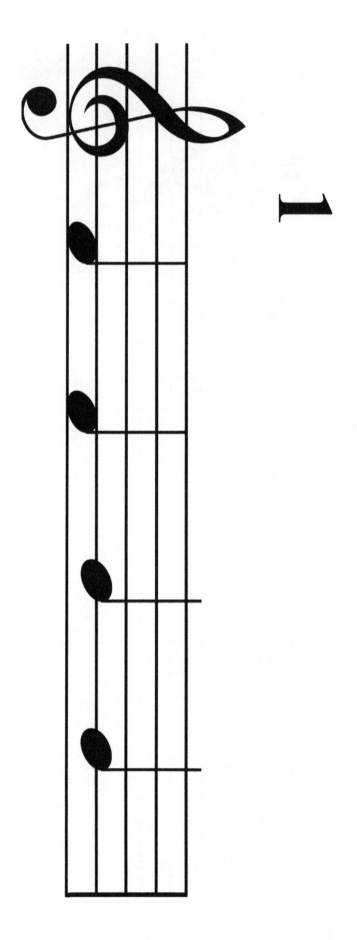

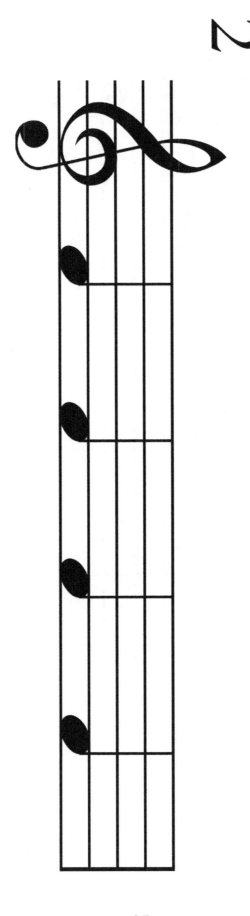

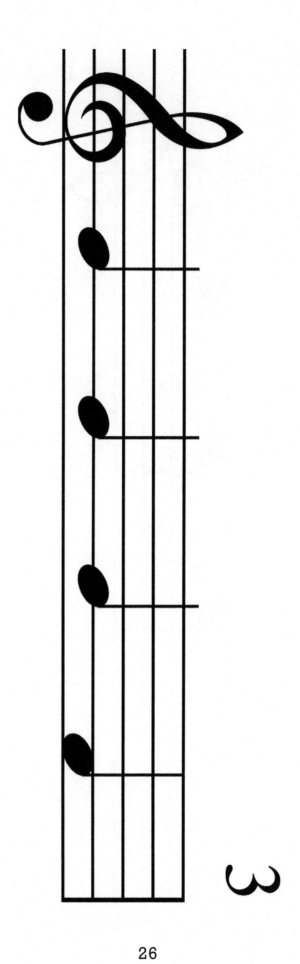

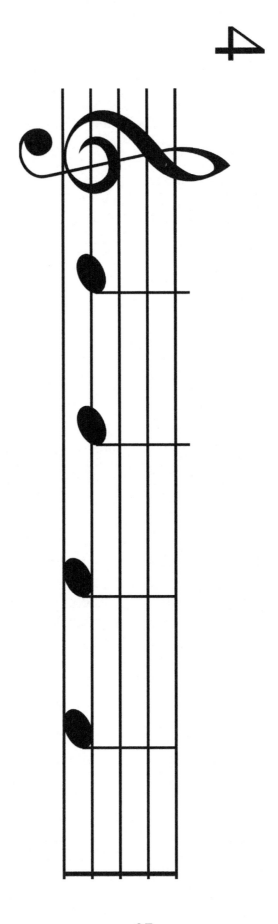

What Can We Do with Five Notes?

Activities use **C D E F G** for treble clef brass. Bass clef equivalents work equally well if needed.

If you have a mixed group using different transpositions (a combination of concert pitch, B flat, E flat and F) then the exercises will either need repeating at the appropriate pitch, or adapting (see below).

> For backing tracks visit:
> **www.musicwild.co.uk** and
> go to the
> **'Wild About Brass'** tab

Activity 1: Echo Playing

*see audio links nos. 4a)i) & 4a)ii) - in Bb, 4b)i) & 4b)ii) - in Eb, and 4c)i) & 4c)ii) - in F. *

- Play phrases of 2 bars in 4/4 using C D E F G (or a bass clef equivalent), for pupils to copy back.

- Start with the lowest note first and the next note up, then gradually move onto higher notes. Once you have reached the highest note come back down in a gradual way.

- Move step wise first, then, if pupils are managing this with ease, move onto phrases containing bigger intervals, such as C and E or D and F, ensuring always that the learners can cope with wider intervals technically.

- If you have multiple transpositions in your group, with a mixture of concert pitch, B flat, E flat and F, then a useful tip is to have a one-note rhythm over two bars as a 'refrain' to return to, on a pitch everyone can play e.g. F for F horns, G for tenor horns and C for trumpets, which you alternate with instrument-specific phrases for each instrument. This two-bar refrain is to ensure that no pupil is asked to wait too long before playing. So, everyone plays the refrain, the teacher plays a phrase for a specific pupil, the pupil copies it, then everyone plays the refrain, and so on. Coping with bass clef and treble clef readers together e.g. trombones and trumpets, tubas and tenor horns is not a problem – you don't have to use the note names, just the sound. For mixed groups of this kind, the audio link will unfortunately not be useable.

(See **Top tips** from 'What Can We Do with Two Notes,' Activity 1: Echo Playing p.9.)

*tracks labelled i) include phrases for pupils to copy back, so facilitate home practice; tracks labelled ii) contain just the backing, giving the teacher more flexibility in lessons.

Activity 2: Improvising - Riff and Rest, Riff and Play

see audio links nos. 5a) - in Bb, 5b) - in Eb, and 5c) - in F. A 'tutti' phrase is included.

- Follow the instructions for Riff and Rest, Riff and Play under 'What Can We Do with Two Notes' p.10, but use all five notes in the phrase that everyone plays (i.e. use C D E F G).

- Advise pupils that they need not use all five notes in their improvisations. It is best to choose just two or three, at least to begin with, and indeed simple improvisations are normally the most effective.

Top tips:

- To help pupils remember which notes they can choose from you can

  a. Do the echo playing activity first

  b. Write each note as a letter on an A4 piece of paper and pin the five pieces of paper in a circle on a wall where everyone can see them. Avoid putting the pieces of paper in a line, as pupils will be tempted to formulate improvisations with the notes exactly in the order they appear on the wall.

- Remember that the process can be broken into small chunks – perhaps a bullet point or two at a time - then returned to the following lesson.

Activity 3: Working Out By Ear

- Sing the first two bars of Frère Jacques starting on C. (For this and subsequent exercises the note names used are those used by 'treble clef' learners. All note names refer to the appropriate transposed pitch).

- Check that pupils recognise this tune. They may know different words, such as 'I Hear Thunder.' You may wish to play the first two bars rather than sing, though remember to avoid giving pupils visual clues such as seeing which valves or slide positions you use.

- Sing or play (giving no visual clues) just the first three notes. Ask pupils if they are all the same or if the notes go higher or lower.

- Having established that the notes go higher, say that the first note is a C, and ask pupils to experiment to find the first three notes. Individual pupils can have a go, or all pupils can try together – quietly - so all have a chance of hearing themselves. When the correct notes have been found, ask all pupils to play the tune so far all together.

- Now sing or play the first four notes. Ask if the fourth was the same as the note before, higher or lower. Having established that it is lower, ask pupils to experiment again to find the right note.

- All play the correct version.

Top tips:

- When checking if pupils are familiar with a tune, be careful how you phrase the question. If you ask pupils 'do you know........?' they may think you mean 'have you played this before?' Ask 'have you heard this tune before' and then play or sing it.

- If a pupil tries an incorrect note, help them to realise what might be wrong, so that that informs their next experimentation. For instance, they may have experimented in the right direction (higher/lower etc.), but too far, or not far enough, so guide them through their next attempt by ensuring that they understand this. This can still be done by questioning rather than telling. You can play the correct version and then what they played, for them to compare.

- Once pupils have found the first four notes this can be turned into an ensemble activity. Ask them to play the fragment on a loop (over and over) whilst you play the tune in its entirety. Plot spoiler – they may fall into the trap of playing C D E C D E rather than repeating the C!

Activity 4: Learning a Tune Without Notation – La Bourrée Occitane

(see audio link as referred to on p.15).

See score for La Bourrée on p.16. For pupils playing five notes refer to the third line of the stave (Part 3).

The first eight bars, or 'A' part

- The process for learning the first eight bars - the 'A' part[2] - will be similar to learning the 'A' part in 'What Can I Do with Two Notes' p.15. Explain to pupils that, as well as tapping their tummies for the note C and their shoulders for D, they will be tapping the tops of their heads for G.

- This time use the words: 'I've had some toast, with jam and butter too,' moving to the top of the head for the G at the end of the phrase.

Tummies..Shoulders.......................Head

I've   had   some   toast   with   jam   and   butt - er   too.

---

[2] In some genres, such as folk music, it is common to label sections of a tune with a letter name.

As before, ask learners to:

    a. Tap the relevant body part whilst saying the fun words (demonstrate first)

    b. Tap relevant body parts whilst *saying* the *note names*

    c. Tap relevant body parts whilst *singing* the *note names*

    d. Tap relevant body parts whilst *thinking* the *note names*

    e. Play that section

- For the rest at the beginning of bar 5 pupils can insert a stamp. This can be moved to 'thinking voice' or retained for performance. 'I've' then becomes the second quaver of the bar, rather than being a full crotchet. Otherwise bars 5 to 8 are the same as for 1 to 4.

The second eight bars, or 'B' part

- Play bars 9 and 10 without pupils seeing your instrument, or sing them. Check pupils have recognised that all the notes are the same apart from the last one. Ask pupils if the last note is higher or lower than the previous notes.

- Having established that the last note is higher, tell pupils that the first note is E, and ask them to play the two bars, experimenting to find the last note. (This is the same process as 'Working Out By Ear' p. 30.) Repeat the process for bars 11 and 12. The words 'jam and butter too' may be used again to help internalise the rhythm.

- For bars 13 and 14, compare them to bars 1 and 2. Play both sections, ensuring again that pupils are using their ears rather than watching for visual clues. Ask pupils to compare the two sections and say what is different. Invite them to play and experiment to find the note in bar 14.

- The first three notes of bar 15 can be likened to Three Blind Mice. Invite pupils to work out the first three notes of Three Blind Mice themselves in the same way they did for Frère Jacques on page 30.

- Next add the dotted rhythm, and the anacrusis in bar 14, by demonstrating and asking pupils to copy.

- Play from the anacrusis in bar 14 to the end, and ask pupils to work out the last 2 notes. Again, you may wish to use prompting questions, such as: 'are the notes the same or different' 'is that note higher or lower' etc.

- Gradually piece together all the bits from the 'B' section, and play several times.

Revise the tune from the beginning. When pupils are confident with all sections, ask them to play their part whilst you play the other parts.

Top tips:

- You can ask pupils to stamp at the beginning of bar 5, and shout 'hoi' on the second beat of bar 12 (as in 'What Can We Do with Two Notes'). This will help to maintain a good pulse, and can either be moved to 'thinking voice' or retained to good effect for performance purposes.

- Unless pupils have access to a recording of the music it will be difficult for them to practise the material at home. If that is the case devote a comparatively small proportion of the lesson to learning the piece and return to it the following week. This will ensure you have enough time to spend on what will be practised for the following lesson.

- Learning the whole tune – even if pupils do have a recording – will take several weeks. However, the process is well worth spending time on – your pupils will benefit enormously in relation to their aural and ensemble skills.

- Using the same principles, arrange your own pieces to suit your pupils.

Supplementary rhythm/ensemble exercise for subdividing the beat:

- Ask pupils to choose words of one syllable and two syllables. Food, pets or pupils' names are good themes. The one syllabled word will be used for crotchets and the two syllabled word for quavers.

- Start pupils off playing crotchets on a note of their choice. Whilst they are doing that, play quavers on the same note, so that the pupils can hear how they fit together.

- Swap roles so that pupils now play the two syllabled word whilst you play the one syllabled word. They will now be subdividing the beat into quavers.

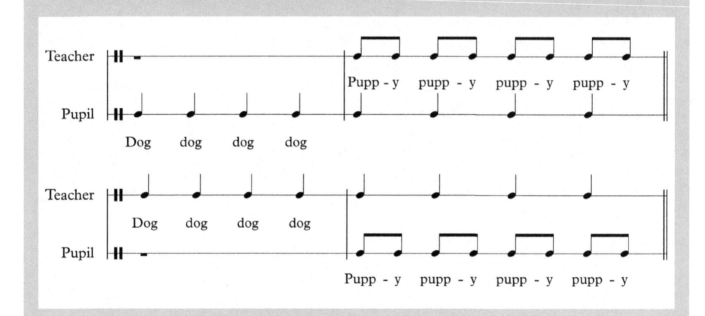

Top tips:

- Let pupils try and work out the correct speed of the quavers themselves, and only intervene as necessary. Advise them not to come in straight away with their quavers, but to listen to how fast the crotchets are going first. Keep the two rhythms going as long as necessary.

- As pupils improve with this, you can introduce subdivision of the crotchet beat into triplet quavers (three syllabled word) and semiquavers (four syllabled word). You can also try different tempi.

- Even if pupils haven't previously heard the word syllable, it is an easy concept for them to learn, and playing the sounds may help them to understand it.

- Articulating syllables of words like 'Dada' can be helpful for tonguing, too.

Activity 5: Arranging and Interpreting – La Bourrée Occitane

- Once your pupils can play their part in La Bourrée Occitane along with the melody, ask them to try articulating notes in two different ways: tenuto and staccato. Invite them to make a judgement on what sounds best. Alternatively try some simple dynamics: pupils could play the first four bars louder than the second four bars and vice versa, then decide which sounds better.

- If playing the piece as an ensemble with all parts invite pupils to think of an introduction. For example, any of the parts could play the 'A' part (bars 1 to 8) three times, with other parts joining in after the first time around.

Activity 6: Notation and Aural

This is similar to Activity 6 in 'What Can I Do with Two Notes,' but uses a wipeable A4 white board with staves on (easily and cheaply available)[3] or an appropriate electronic device.

- Ask each pupil to write a group of four notes on the board. You may wish to use all five notes or just C and D, or any three or any four. Start simple!

- Label everyone's pattern of four notes: Mr Li's, Ayeesha's, Celina's etc. One person can write a pattern of four notes, the next person name them, the next person play them. Then move on, ensuring that every pupil has written, named and played.

- Play one of the patterns and ask pupils to work out which one you played. Ensure pupils can't see your slide or fingers, so stand behind them, or sing the pattern. Pupils need to use their ears to work it out, not their eyes. The individual who identifies the correct pattern first gets the chance to play a pattern for the rest of the group to identify. Ensure all have a go at this, so you can use the rule that if a pupil has already answered one, got it right and played, they should miss the next turn(s). With individual pupils, teacher and pupil can write two groups of four notes each.

Points to Note:

By writing the notes down themselves, pupils achieve a thorough understanding of how one note is differentiated from another. It also helps you to check that they have understood which symbol represents which sound.

When pupils first try this activity, you may wish to have the notes displayed in order somewhere, with relevant letters, fingerings or slide positions written above. Pupils can refer to this to work out the patterns written down. However, ensure that this is just a transitional stage.

[3] For instance: www.musicroom.com/product/musch74085/wipe-clean-music-board-landscape-edition

What Can We Do with Eight Notes?

Activities use the scale of **C major** (appropriately transposed) as an example. Other keys, for example concert B flat major for trombone, can be used.

For backing tracks visit: www.musicwild.co.uk and go to the 'Wild About Brass' tab

Activity 1: Echo Playing

*see audio links nos. 6a)i) & 6a)ii) - in Bb, 6b)i) & 6b)ii) - in Eb, and 6c)i) & 6c)ii) - in F. ***

- Play phrases for pupils to copy back, as described in 'What Can We Do with Two Notes' and 'What Can We Do with Five Notes' pages 9 and 28.

* tracks labelled i) include phrases for pupils to copy back, so facilitate home practice; tracks labelled ii) contain just the backing, giving the teacher more flexibility in lessons.

Activity 2: Improvising a Melody

- Do a little echo playing as in the previous activity, to remind pupils which notes will be used in the improvisations – notes from the scale of C.

- Play a 2 bar 'questioning' phrase in 4/4, and invite the pupil to answer with a 2 bar phrase. Explain that they need to finish on the key note if possible as this will result in a 'complete' feel. Demonstrate this. You may wish to refer to the key note as the home note. Invite the pupil to have a few goes to try and achieve this. In a small group pupils can take turns – play a questioning phrase for each pupil, and let each one have a turn at answering.

- The pupil is now going to play the 'question' and you the 'answer.' Count four beats in for the pupil. This is slightly harder for the learner, as they have to generate the raw material. However, pupils no longer need to finish on the key note. When you answer include aspects of the learner's phrase in yours. Point this out. It's useful for the pupil to understand that within a piece of music there will be variation but also some common factors. (In a small group take turns, as above.)

- Now the pupil is going to play both the 'question' and the 'answer.' Count the pupil four beats in. It's helpful to remind the learner that this is like a conversation. So far one of you has asked a question and one of you has answered. Now the learner is taking on both roles in the conversation.

- Ask the pupil to count *themselves* in, either out loud or with thinking voice, and to play a whole tune: question and answer. (It is helpful for the pupil to count 1 2 3 out loud, but to breathe or say 'mmm' on the count 4 in order to get ready to play). The learner is now equipped with all the tools they need to practise this at home.

Top tips:

- It may take a little while to get to the last bullet point, so until then just devote bite sized pieces to the activity in the lesson. A bullet point a week normally works well.

- If pupils continue to struggle with phrase length, return to the improvisation activity described in 'What Can We Do with Two Notes' and 'What Can We Do with Five Notes' pages 10 and 29 to help them internalise the appropriate number of bars.

- This activity can be revisited as progress is made, and new tonalities are available. It is a very effective way to embed the learning of a new scale.

Activity 3: Working Out By Ear

Happy Birthday

- Think about how much of the tune you want to work on with your pupils. The first one or two phrases is good for this stage, i.e. after the first or the second 'to you.' Any more of the melody becomes more challenging, so you may want to save this till later, or use for an extension activity with pupils who are managing particularly well.

- Starting on C, sing that part of the tune, asking pupils to simultaneously sign the shape of the melody in a simple way – hand out in front, keeping it to the same level when a pitch is repeated, lifting higher when the pitch rises, and dropping lower when it falls. Sign with pupils to begin with.

- Repeat with you singing but not signing. Pupils continue to sign.

- Repeat *without* you singing. Pupils sign. (The tune is now only going on in their heads.)

- If pupils are in a group, repeat but without them being able to see each other. You can ask them to face away from each other. This enables you to check that each pupil has understood, knows the tune, and can discriminate accurately between pitches.

- Sing or play (without them seeing your fingers), just the first four notes. Ask pupils:

  '...............how many notes are the same before it changes?'

  '...............does the tune go higher or lower at that point?'

  '...............by a lot or a little?'

  '...............what happens next?'

- Give pupils the first note and ask them to experiment until they have found the first four notes. When the correct notes have been found, all pupils play the tune so far.

- Now sing or play the first six notes and ask pupils about the shape of the melody. They will probably have indicated with their hand gestures earlier that the interval is bigger after '_day' than it was after 'Happy.' Once the shape has been established ask pupils to experiment until they have found the right notes. Advise them to keep playing from the beginning, as to do otherwise can land them in the wrong key!

- If all is going well, try as far as the first twelve notes using the same principles. Pupils will need to spot that the notes for the second 'Happy Birthday' are the same as for the first, but that the interval after the second 'Happy Birthday' is wider. The question: 'does the tune go higher by a lot or a little' may be useful here.

- Pupils can be asked to practise this at home now, with just a reminder of what the first note is.

Top tips:

- When asking pupils to practise a tune which they are working out by ear, emphasise that they just need to experiment – the correct notes may well not be found immediately. Remind them of the questions they need to ask themselves: 'is the next note the same or different? If it is the same, how many notes are the same before the pitch changes? If it is different is the next note higher or lower? Is it different by a lot or a little?' Remind them not to go on to the next bit of the piece until they are satisfied each bit is correct, to avoid inadvertently changing key. Reassure them that this is a painstaking, sometimes slow, process – it is not their own lack of ability that makes the process slow!

- When working out by ear with a group, and on more than just a short phrase or two, you can ask pupils to take it in turns to work out the notes - one pupil can work out the first few notes, then all play, then the next person plays from the beginning but works out the next bit as well, all play the notes so far, then onto the next pupil, and so on.

Point to note:

For more advanced pupils, working out the whole tune is a good way to introduce B flats. Even if only the first part of the tune is learned at this stage, the activity can be profitably revisited when B flat is learned later, so that the melody can be completed.

Activity 4: Learning a Tune Without Notation – La Bourrée Occitane

(see audio link as referred to on p.15).

See score on p. 16. Pupils will be playing line 2.

Some preliminary exercises to familiarise learners with features from the tune:

- Play the scale of C major all together. Use a pattern from the tune to play on each note, for example, the rhythm from bars 3 and 4, or bar 9. An advanced student may even be able to play the melodic feature from bar 9 on each note of the scale, i.e.   C   EC E |D   FD   F |E   GE   G etc.

- Play a rhythm from the tune on every note of a C major arpeggio – arpeggios feature highly in the tune. This can be a good way of introducing arpeggios, or can reinforce them if they are already learnt.

- Do some Echo Playing, as in Activity 1 – first 2 bars in 2/4 at a time, then 4 bars at a time. Concentrate particularly on starting from the top note of the scale and working down, as is featured in the tune, for example from the end of bar 2. Include next door notes, leaps of a third e.g. G down to E and a fourth e.g. G down to D. Having achieved this, learners will be in a good position to work out the notes when you play the melody.

Learning the tune – the first eight bars, or 'A' part.

N.B. Learners will have the opportunity to hear the melody many times before playing it, whilst still being actively involved.

- Teach the accompanying rhythm (see below). Learners can clap, with a stamp on the first beat of bar 6. Once they have it, play the melody simultaneously with them. (The stamp may be retained once pupils can play the melody if wished.)

- Teach a simple accompaniment to be played on their instruments: in crotchets, C x 4, G x 4, C x 4, G x 4. Again, when they have this, play the melody simultaneously with them.

- Teach the learners to play a short fragment of the tune (see below). This is obviously just an arpeggio with two different rhythms. They now need to play their two excerpts whilst you play the tune. In order to help them know when to play and when to listen, you can first play with them, and sing the bits in between.

- Ask pupils to play progressively longer bits, as below. To help pupils learn bars 3 to 4, and 7 to 8, give the starting note and teach as for echo playing. Then play that segment all together on a loop (over and over). Once they have it, ask pupils to piece the bits together as below, and play whilst you play the tune in its entirety.

- You now just have the anacruses to add at the ends of bars 2 and 6.

- Play through the 'A' section a couple of times.

Learning the tune – the second eight bars, or 'B' part.

- Refer to the cuckoo-like nature of the figure in bar 9. Teach pupils how to do this, oscillating between G and E.

- Ask pupils to play the precise notes in bar 9 by starting on the lower note and adding the dotted rhythm.

- Teach bar 10 by asking pupils to repeat the figure up one note. You may wish to introduce the term 'sequence.'

- Put bar 9 and bar 10 together, repeat the notes from bar 9, and add a D. They now have bars 9 to 12.

- Play from bar 13 to the first beat of bar 14 to your pupils. They will probably spot that bar 13 is the same as the beginning. Now the D just needs adding. If pupils managed well with echo playing including the interval of a fourth, ask them to work the note out. If not, and or you want to keep a brisk pace to the lesson, just let them know what the note is.

- For the final two bars, give the first note and teach the notes as for echo playing (as you did in bars 3 to 4, and 7 to 8). You now just need to add the anacrusis at the end of bar 14.

- Piece all the bits together and play through the 'B' section a couple of times.

Play the whole tune together with your pupils. Some revision may be needed – the 'A' part won't be thoroughly internalised yet.

Ask pupils to play the tune whilst you play the other parts, including Part 1.

Top tips:

- You can ask pupils to stamp at the beginning of bar 5, and shout 'hoi' on the second beat of bar 12 (as in 'What Can We Do with Two Notes' and 'What Can We Do with Five Notes').

- To help pupils memorise the structure of the tune, compare it to a conversation between a toddler and a parent, for example:

  — Bars 1 and 2 – the child demanding something (e.g. 'I want some sweets!')
  — Bars 3 (with up-beat) and 4 – the parent refusing
  — Bars 5 and 6 – the child demanding more forcefully – with a stamp
  — Bars 7 and 8 – the parent refusing again
  — Bars 9 to 14 – the child asking again, this time lengthily and repetitively, perhaps more politely (e.g. 'Can I have some, can I have some, can I have some please?)
  — Bars 15 (with up-beat) and 16 – the parent giving the final answer (e.g. 'Well yes, but after tea').

- Unless pupils have access to a recording of the music it will be difficult for them to practise the material at home. If that is the case devote a comparatively small proportion of the lesson to learning the piece and return to it the following week. This will ensure you have enough time to spend on what will be practised for the following lesson.

- Using the same principles, arrange your own pieces to suit your pupils.

Activity 5: Arranging and Interpreting – La Bourrée Occitane

- Ask one of the group to indicate louds and softs of their choice with a hand gesture whilst the others play the tune. Hands close together for soft, hands far apart for loud works well. In an individual lesson you could be the one playing and following directions. Try and ensure that all have a go, or if it is an individual lesson, that the pupil has tried a few different versions. Encourage pupils to discuss the different versions, in a positive way. Ask them what went particularly well, and allow the pupil directing to suggest what they might do differently next time.

Point to note:

This activity is a lot of fun. There is joy and some humour to be found by your friends responding with sound to the gestures you make! Ensure that, after the novelty wears off, pupils are really developing their musical decision making, in other words, that they are listening, evaluating, and thinking about their intended sound.

- Ask pupils to see if there are any places in the melody where slurs would sound good – perhaps the pairs of quavers in bar 1 or bar 3 for example. Invite them to experiment.
- If playing the piece as an ensemble with all parts invite pupils to think of an introduction. For example, any of the parts could play the 'A' part (bars 1 to 8) three times, with other parts joining in after the first time around.

Activity 6: Notation and Aural

- Repeat the activity as described in 'What Can We Do with Five Notes' p.36 this time using notes from a complete scale.

Appendix

Advice for teaching the activities online

At the time of writing **Listen, Think, Create**, many lessons are delivered online. This is largely due to covid-19 restrictions, though online teaching is sometimes the only way to deliver lessons if, for instance, pupils live in a remote area. Online teaching presents some challenges. I have outlined below how these might apply to the activities in this book, and suggested ways of dealing with any issues arising.

Echo Playing

On the whole there is not much problem with echo playing. You as the teacher will experience a gap after you have finished playing a phrase, but this won't be experienced by the pupil.
When using the supplementary exercise for differentiating pitch (p. 10), there will be a gap between you moving pitch and the pupil moving their hand. This is easy to deal with as long as you expect it and don't try to fluctuate between pitches too quickly.

Improvising

— **Riff and Rest, Riff and Play (What Can We Do with Two/Five Notes? pages 10 and 29).** This is not practical for online lessons, though pupils will be able to practise it at home with the online resource. This will benefit them in aiding the development of pulse and feel for phrase length. In lessons you can use the improvising a melody activity (see below). For this stage of playing it is probably best to just ask pupils to improvise the answering phrase. They can still aim to finish on the 'home note' or tonic even with just two notes.

— **Improvising a Melody (What Can We Do with Eight Notes? p.37).** This is manageable, though there will be a gap experienced by the person playing the questioning phrase after they have finished – you in the first instance, but subsequently the pupil, so it is good to make them aware of this. Using the **Riff and Rest, Riff and Play** resource (see above) in their practice will ensure pupils are able to maintain a steady pulse and internalise the correct phrase length.

Working Out By Ear

This is absolutely fine online. However, asking pupils to sign lower/higher pitches whilst you sing the melody (as in **'What Can We Do with Eight Notes?' p. 39**) is problematic due to the time lag. Stick to making good use of questions, such as: 'does the tune stay on the same note, go higher or lower at this point?'

Learning a Tune Without Notation

Generally this is absolutely fine. Playing the tune whilst pupils play accompanying parts may be confusing for you due to the time lag, so you may want to mute them. In any case, pupils can make use of the audio resource to practice playing with other parts simultaneously. Learning the tune in the ways specified for **'What Can We Do with Eight Notes?' p.41** may be problematic due to the (normally helpful) strategy of getting pupils to play something whilst you play the tune. Instead try to ensure pupils get a clear idea of the tune as a whole by playing it to them, inviting them to comment on any repeated bits and other structural details. Also ensure features of the tune are included in preliminary exercises so that they will be quickly spotted. Then teach the tune by echo playing, using short, then increasingly longer fragments.

Arranging and Interpreting

Activities for single parts of **'La Bourrée'** are fine, though of course those requiring all ensemble players to be present are not. The activity for deciding dynamics in **'What Can We Do with Eight Notes?' p.45** is difficult. Instead, simply ask pupils to experiment by playing the tune in several different ways (i.e. with different dynamics) and evaluate the results.

Notation and Aural

This is fine, just ensure that you and the pupils are looking at equivalent things, i.e. the same note patterns in the same order. For **'What Can We Do with Five/Eight Notes?' (pages 36/45)** you may want to adapt that part of the activity which refers to pupils writing down their own notes.

Supplementary rhythm exercises

The aural/rhythm exercise for differentiating between crotchets and minims (p.13) is fine, but the exercise for subdividing the beat (p.34) is best saved for face-to-face lessons.

Printed in Great Britain
by Amazon